The Fisherman's Guide to Life

The Fisherman's Guide to Life

Nine Timeless Principles Based On the Lessons of Fishing

Compiled and Edited by Criswell Freeman

WALNUT GROVE PRESS
Nashville, TN 37205

ISBN 1-887655-30-1

The ideas expressed in this book are not, in all cases, exact quotations, as some have been edited for clarity and brevity. In all cases, the author has attempted to maintain the speaker's original intent. In some cases, material for this book was obtained from secondary sources, primarily print media. While every effort was made to ensure the accuracy of these sources, the accuracy cannot be guaranteed. For additions, deletions, corrections or clarifications in future editions of this text, please write WALNUT GROVE PRESS.

Printed in the United States of America
Cover Design by Mary Mazer
Typesetting & Page Layout by Sue Gerdes
Edited by Alan Ross and Angela Beasley
6 7 8 9 10 •   99 00 01

ACKNOWLEDGMENTS
The author gratefully acknowledges the helpful support of Angela Beasley, Dick and Mary Freeman, and Mary Susan Freeman.

For Carlisle Beasley

Great Fisherman, Greater Friend

Table of Contents

Introduction 13

Lesson 1: Carpe Diem..................................... 15
The Trip Is Brief — Enjoy It

Lesson 2: Lifetime Learning 29
*The Ultimate Lure Is the Mind
Of the Fisherman*

Lesson 3: The Tackle Box 53
*The Better the Lure,
The Bigger the Fish*

Lesson 4: Patience 63
You Can't Hurry a Fish

Lesson 5: Respect for Nature 81
Leave the River As You Found It

Lesson 6: Silence.. 105
Quiet Waters Are Wise Counsel

Lesson 7: Humility 121
You Can't Hook 'Em All

Lesson 8: Optimism 133
Cast Hope upon the Waters

Lesson 9: Gratitude 149
*Every Day Spent Fishing Is a Day
To Give Thanks*

Introduction

Our most profound lessons, first learned in childhood, must be relearned again and again throughout life. We know the fundamental principles all too well: fairness, honesty, optimism and love, to name a few. But in the wake of the daily grind, we forget. The universal human dilemma is this: Perspective is a perishable commodity.

Fishing restores perspective. When we escape to the solitude of quiet waters, the day's fleeting troubles seem to evaporate into the mist; in the presence of Nature, spiritual order is restored.

The observant angler has many lessons to learn, and this book addresses a few of them. Utilizing the words of renowned fishermen, writers and philosophers, each principle is examined in light of its application to fishing and, more importantly, its application to life.

Whether we visit the neighborhood pond, the bubbling brook, or the open seas, the message of the waters is the same: Be prepared, be patient, and enjoy the moment. Some days the fish will bite, some days they won't. In the grand scheme, the size of a day's catch isn't very important. But whenever we go down to the water and rediscover an important lesson about life — sure enough, that's a keeper.

LESSON 1: CARPE DIEM

The Trip Is Brief — Enjoy It

A good fishing trip, like a well-cooked meal or a well-lived life, always ends a little too soon. The Roman poet Horace understood the temporal nature of earthly things when he wrote, "Carpe diem, quam minimum credula postero!" Translation: "Seize the day, put no trust in the morrow!"

The wise angler understands that every trip to the water is, in a sense, his last. Because nature is constantly changing, no man fishes the same water twice — even if he spends a lifetime casting into a single small pond. The fish, the water and the weather are in a state of constant flux; more importantly, the angler himself is changing with each passing day.

The existential philosopher Albert Camus wrote, "Real generosity toward the future lies in giving all to the present." And so it is with fishing. The trip is altogether too brief, so why not savor every moment?

Carpe Diem

Angling is the way to round out a happy life.
Charles K. Fox

If you wish to be happy for eight days,
kill your pig and eat it. If you wish to be happy
for a lifetime, learn to fish.
Chinese Proverb

For the true angler, fishing produces
a deep, unspoken joy, born of longing for that
which is quiet and peaceful, and fostered by
an inbred love of communing with nature.
Thaddeus Norris

After all these years, I still feel like a boy
when I'm on a stream or lake.
Jimmy Carter

No life is so happy and so pleasant as the life of the well-govern'd angler.

Izaak Walton

Carpe Diem

When is the best season of the year
to go a-fishing? When you feel like it
and can leave home and business.

Charles Bradford

The two best times to go fishing are
when it's raining and when it's not.

Fisherman's Saying

Fishing seems to be the favorite form
of loafing.

Ed Howe

A bad day fishing still beats
a good day working.

Fisherman's Saying

If fishing interferes with your business, give up your business.

Sparse Grey Hackle

One thing becomes clearer as one gets
older and one's fishing experience increases,
and that is the paramount importance
of one's fishing companions.

John Ashley-Cooper

I now believe that fishing is
far more important than the fish.

Arnold Gingrich

Why do people go fishing?
Some say they fish to get fish.
This is obviously false.

John W. Randolph

I have fished through fishless days that
I remember happily and without regret.

Roderick Haig-Brown

Every intelligent sportsman knows that
the greatest rewards of hunting and fishing
are irresistible.

Ted Trueblood

'Tis not all of fishing to fish.

Izaak Walton

The gods do not deduct
from a man's allotted
span the hours spent in
fishing.

Babylonian Proverb

Fishing is the chance to wash one's soul
with pure air, with the rush of a brook or
with the shimmer of the sun on blue water.

Herbert Hoover

I have experienced such simple joy
in the trivial matters of fishing and sport
formerly as might inspire the muse
of Homer or Shakespeare.

Henry David Thoreau

Nothing can bring you peace but yourself.

Ralph Waldo Emerson

Angling is somewhat like poetry.

Izaak Walton

The angler is never a has-been.
He enjoys a lifetime of participation which
continues through noon, then on into the
sunset, and even into the eventide of life.

Charles K. Fox

Happiness is not a state to arrive at,
but a manner of traveling.

Samuel Johnson

Fish come and go, but it is the memory of afternoons on the stream that endure.

E. Donnall Thomas

Of all the world's enjoyments,
That ever valued were;
There's none of our employments
With fishing can compare.

Thomas D'Urfey

No fisherman ever fishes as much
as he wants to.

Geoffrey Norman

Angling is not only a most agreeable
and delightful amusement — it also imparts
health and long life.

Palmer Hackle, Esq.

If a man fishes hard,
      what is he going to do easy?

Roy Blount, Jr.

Ignorant men don't know what good
      they hold in their hands until they've
            flung it away.

Sophocles

It is now, and in this world that we must live.

André Gide

The trout do not rise
in the cemetery, so you
better do your fishing
while you are still able.

Sparse Grey Hackle

LESSON 2: LIFETIME LEARNING

The Ultimate Lure Is the Mind Of the Fisherman

In the days before hooks, lines, rods, and reels, a fisherman relied on creativity for his daily catch. His tackle consisted of such unlikely items as sticks, spears, animal parts, even spider webs. And he caught fish.

Today, quality tackle is available to every angler whose income is sufficient to support his habit. But the most important lure remains the knowledge and ingenuity of the fisherman.

For the uninitiated, catching fish is a simple business: bait a hook, drop it in the water, see what happens. The seasoned angler knows better. Fish are not so much caught as they are outsmarted.

Some fishermen, through a commitment to lifetime learning, transform sport into art. The following quotations celebrate those anglers who, like their prey, never stop schooling.

No man ever became wise by chance.

Seneca

No man is born an Artist nor an Angler.

Izaak Walton

The doer alone learneth.

Nietzsche

Books can't make you a good fisherman,
but they can make you a better one.

Fisherman's Saying

A man should never stop learning,
even on his last day.

Maimonides

A man, though wise, should never
be ashamed of learning more.

Sophocles

All veteran anglers have their tricks
of the trade ... usually you have to fish
a long time to pick them up.

Wheeler Johnson

It's what you learn after you know it all
that counts.

Harry Truman

Learning to catch fish is not difficult,
but becoming reasonably expert at it does
require time and study.

A. J. McClane

Anglers are not born, they are made by
circumstances, and sometimes it takes a long
time to get the right circumstances together.

John W. Randolph

Casting is not the end of learning.
In fact, it is only the beginning.

Geoffrey Norman

I am still learning.

Michelangelo's Motto

Nature is always hinting at us.

Robert Frost

The great charm of fly-fishing is that
we are always learning.

Theodore Gordon

I grow old ever learning many things.

Solon

One of the charms of the sport
is its infinite complexity. The wood has a
depth and richness to reward a lifetime
of quiet, perspective searching.

Roderick Haig-Brown

A man, though wise, should never
be ashamed of learning more.

Sophocles

The years teach much
which the days never know.
Ralph Waldo Emerson

Education is hanging on
until you've caught on.
Robert Frost

Anyone who stops learning is old,
whether at twenty or eighty.
Henry Ford

A whale ship was my Yale and my Harvard.
Herman Melville

Remember that angling is an art,
and an art worthy the knowledge
and practice of a wise man.
Izaak Walton

Angling may be said
to be like mathematics in
that it can never
fully be learnt.

Izaak Walton

B eyond every bend in a stream lies a new
fishing challenge, for no pool, riffle or rapids
is just like the previous one.

Dick Sternberg

Y ou cannot step twice into the same river,
for other waters are continually flowing in.

Heraclitus

E very lesson you learn, no matter where
you learn it, transfers to all other rivers,
no matter where you fish.

Dave Hughes

Man can learn a lot from fishing. When the fish are biting, no problem in the world is big enough to be remembered.

Oa Battista

To learn is a natural pleasure not confined
to philosophers, but common to all men.

Aristotle

To be a successful angler, one must have
a good knowledge of fish, for to understand
the quarry is to defeat him.

Tiny Bennett

Successful anglers are sticklers for doing
everything precisely right, because they know
a slight difference in technique can make
a big difference in the catch.

Ted Trueblood

Successful hunters and fishermen are
precise observers of the world around them.
They have to be in order to be successful.

George Reiger

Knowledge comes, but wisdom lingers.

Alfred Lord Tennyson

A man that goeth to the River for his pleasure must understand the Sun and the Wind, the Moon and the Stars, and set forth his tackle accordingly.

Thomas Barker

If you take your boat into the shallow waters,
know where the stumps are.

Fisherman's Saying

Nothing is ever simple about fish,
whether it's catching them
or understanding them.

A. J. McClane

When, I wonder, are folks going to learn
that it is a dangerous thing to attempt to lay
down hard and fast rules about fishing?

John Alden Knight

A fishing notebook
is invaluable, and
all serious anglers
should keep one.

Ted Trueblood

The wary angler in the
winding brook, knows
the fish and where
to bait his hook.

Ovid

When there are no fish
in one spot, cast your
hook in another.

Chinese Proverb

Four-fifths of the earth's surface is covered
with water, but only five percent of that
is good fishing.

Geoffrey Norman

The secret of successful angling depends
on learning the kind of water the fish prefer,
and then concentrating on it.

Ted Trueblood

If you want to catch fish,
you better be fishing in the right pond.

Old Saying

Most of the world is covered by water.
A fisherman's job is simple:
Pick out the best parts.

Charles F. Waterman

The best fisherman in the
world can't catch them
if they aren't there.

Anthony Acerrano

Ten percent of the water holds ninety percent of the fish.

Dave Hughes

Ten percent of the fishermen catch ninety percent of the fish.

Fisherman's Saying

The hardest part of fishing is learning
to read water.

Geoffrey Norman

You can't learn any stream by heart
in less than three seasons.

Arnold Gingrich

The first principle of reading water is this:
Fish are found at the edges of things.

Charles F. Waterman

Every fishing water has its secrets.
A river or a lake is not a dead thing. It has
beauty and wisdom and content. And to yield
up these mysteries, it must be fished
with more than hooks.

Zane Grey

Anybody can see the weeds. It takes a little
practice to notice the less obvious features.

Charles F. Waterman

Learn to visualize the lake
without the water.

Jim Chapralis

The man who keeps everything locked up
in his heart will know far less than he
who compares notes with his fellows.

Theodore Gordon

Men learn while they teach.

Seneca

I can learn from anyone, but I do not stop
at that. I go on trying to learn from myself.

Zane Grey

Give a man a fish and you feed him for a day. Teach him to fish and you feed him for a lifetime.

Ancient Proverb

Any man who pits his intelligence against a fish and loses has it coming.

John Steinbeck

LESSON 3: THE TACKLE BOX

The Better the Lure,
The Bigger the Fish

Scottish-born author Thomas Carlyle wrote, "Man is a tool-using animal. Without tools he is nothing; with tools, he is all." These words are particularly true as they apply to the art of angling.

The serious fisherman understands that success on the water begins long before the first cast. Success begins with the acquisition and organization of a well-stocked tackle box. The fisherman who wishes to improve his catch must first improve his tools. In fishing, as in life, preparation is the better part of luck.

Prepare your tackle.
   When you hook a big fish, it is impossible
      to retie a knot or change a leader.

Jim Chapralis

Good people order and arrange.

Confucius

The secret to success in life is for a man to
be ready for his opportunity when it comes.

Benjamin Disraeli

The joys of fishing are not confined
   to the hours near the water.

Herbert Hoover

A good fisherman can secure many regenerative hours in winter, polishing up the rods and reels.

Herbert Hoover

A fisherman will spend almost as much time in tackle shops as he will upon a trout stream.

William Hjortsberg

Fishing equipment is fun.

Roderick Haig-Brown

If you need a piece of equipment, make it
as light as possible. If you don't need it,
leave it home.

Sparse Grey Hackle

If you need a piece of equipment and
don't buy it, you pay for it even though
you don't have it.

Henry Ford

Your outfit may be elaborate, or it may be
a cane pole. Fortunately, the size of your kit
is no indication of the pleasure you derive.

Jack Randolph

A good rod is without doubt
the Angler's chief requisite.

Hardy Brothers Catalogue, 1886

One of the turning points
of my life was when I got
my first bait-casting outfit.

Jimmy Carter

He that would catch Fish
must venture his Bait.

Ben Franklin

You can catch your next fish
with a piece of the last.

Oliver Wendell Holmes

Venture a small fish to catch a great one.

Thomas Fuller

The reason life
sometimes seems dull
is because we do not
perceive the importance
and excitement
of getting bait.

Henry Van Dyke

It is a tried and true axiom that as
a fisherman grows more specialized and
refined in his pursuits, the equipment
he needs becomes increasingly
complex and varied.

William J. Hjortsberg

Unless you have a ritual for getting your
tackle box ready, no one will regard you
as a serious fisherman.

John W. Randolph

LESSON 4: PATIENCE
You Can't Hurry a Fish

Nature marches to the beat of its own drum. And fish bite when they're ready, not before. An angler's frustration will not force a fish to bite. Nor will his worry.

Since one can't hurry a fish, angling inevitably becomes a lesson in patience and persistence. Once a fisherman has done his best, the rest must be left up to his prey.

So remember: If the fish aren't biting, let them not bite. But keep fishing. The next cast may hook the big one.

The greatest fishing
secret ever?
Patience.

Donald Jack Anderson

Be patient and calm — for no one can catch fish in anger.

Herbert Hoover

He that is slow to wrath
is of great understanding.

Proverbs 14: 29

God helps those who persevere.

The Koran

No great thing is created suddenly.

Epictetus

All human power is a compound
of time and patience.

Honoré De Balzac

There is a final moment of unyielding patience which, in Angling, so often makes the difference between fish and no fish.

Sparse Grey Hackle

It does not matter how slowly you go,
so long as you do not stop.

Confucius

Patience is the companion of wisdom.

St. Augustine

Angling is an art worthy the knowledge
and patience of a wise man.

Izaak Walton

You can't catch fish on a dry line.

Fisherman's Saying

If you want fish, fish.

German Proverb

Adopt the pace of nature;
her secret is patience.

Ralph Waldo Emerson

All you need to be a fisherman is patience and a worm.

Herb Shriver

Persistence, for the fisherman, is a virtue that transcends patience.

A. J. McClane

The hasty angler loses the fish.

Fisherman's Saying

Never cut what you can untie.

Joseph Joubert

Don't clean your fish before you catch them.

Fisherman's Saying

A fish is larger for being lost.

Japanese Proverb

Patience is bitter but its fruit is sweet.

Jean Jacques Rousseau

Genius is nothing but a greater aptitude
for patience.

Ben Franklin

So frequent the casts. So seldom a strike.

Arnold Gingrich

Have patience with all things,
but first of all with yourself.

St. Frances of Sales

Be content: The sea hath fish enough.

Thomas Fuller

Patience is power.

Chinese Proverb

God, grant me the serenity to accept
the things I cannot change, the courage
to change the things I can, and the wisdom
to know the difference.

Reinhold Niebuhr

To do nothing is sometimes a good remedy.

Hippocrates

There is a time to fish
and a time to dry the nets.

Fisherman's Saying

There is a rhythm to an angler's life
and a rhythm to his year.

Nick Lyons

A thousand fishing trips go by,
indistinguishable from one another,
and then suddenly one comes along
that is fatefully perfect.

A. J. McClane

Nothing happens unless first a dream.

Carl Sandburg

A fisherman has many dreams.
Sometimes dreams, even those of a fisherman,
come true.

Zane Grey

There is a distinct similarity between cattle
and casters in that each regards the grass as
being greener on the other side of the fence.

Charles K. Fox

The best fish swim deep.

Thomas Fuller

Only the game fish swims upstream.

John Trotwood Moore

I knew an old fisherman who said he
enjoyed the times when the fish weren't
biting, for then he had time to see and
hear all the things he would miss
if he were too busy hauling in fish.

Archibald Rutledge

There's no taking trout with dry breeches.

Cervantes

Character is that which can do
without success.

Ralph Waldo Emerson

If you want to catch more fish,
use more hooks.

George Allen

Luck affects everything;
let your hook always be
cast. In the stream where
you least expect it,
there will be fish.

Ovid

LESSON 5: RESPECT FOR NATURE

Leave the River As You Found It

Zane Grey wrote, "If I fished only to capture fish, my fishing trips would have ended long ago." And so it is with most anglers. The thrill of the catch is often overshadowed by nature's breathtaking grandeur.

Fishermen become a part of the waters they fish. As naturalist John Muir observed, "When one tugs on a single thing in nature, one finds it attached to the rest of the world."

Only when we approach the water with respect do we gain its fullest measure of enjoyment. The fish aren't always biting, but Mother Nature is always watching. So we'd best behave ourselves.

We can never have enough of Nature.

Henry David Thoreau

God is making the world, and the show
is so grand and beautiful and exciting that
I never have been able to study any other.

John Muir

I have never been happier, more exhilarated,
at peace, inspired, and aware of the grandeur
of the universe and the greatness of God
than when I find myself in a natural setting
not much changed from the way
He made it.

Jimmy Carter

Nature is the art of God.

Dante

One of the great charms
of angling is that of all
the sports, it affords the
best opportunity to enjoy
the wonders and beauty
of nature.

J. J. Manley

In the wilderness is the salvation of mankind.
Henry David Thoreau

Everything in excess is opposed to nature.
Hippocrates

True wisdom consists in not departing
from nature and in molding our conduct
to her laws and model.
Seneca

Though we travel the world over to find
the beautiful, we must carry it with us
or we find it not.
Ralph Waldo Emerson

Fishing is more than fish; it is the vitalizing
lure to outdoor life.

Herbert Hoover

Love of nature is a common language that
can transcend political and social boundaries.

Jimmy Carter

It seems to me that the earth may
be borrowed but not bought. It may
be used but not owned. We are tenants,
not possessors, lovers and not masters.

Marjorie Kinnan Rawlings

Man masters nature not by force
but by understanding.

Jacob Bronowski

You can't fight nature and win.

Ted Trueblood

Nothing is evil which is according to nature.

Marcus Aurelius

Deviation from nature is deviation
from happiness.

Samuel Johnson

See Nature, and
through her, God.

Henry David Thoreau

Every river that flows is good and has
something worthy to be loved.

Henry Van Dyke

Perhaps fishing is, for me,
only an excuse to be near rivers.

Roderick Haig-Brown

All our Concord waters have two colors
   at least: one when viewed at a distance,
   and another, more proper, close at hand.
                              Henry David Thoreau

Nature is an unlimited broadcasting station
   through which God speaks to us every hour
             — if we will only tune in.
                         George Washington Carver

All but beauty will pass — beauty will
   never die. No, not even when the earth and
      the sun have died will beauty perish.
            It will live on in the stars.
                         William Robinson Leigh

Wherever the trout are,
it's beautiful.

Thomas Masaryck

When the Creator made all things,
He first made the fishes in the Big Water.

American Indian Legend

A lake is the landscape's most beautiful
and expressive feature. It is earth's eye,
looking into which the beholder measures
the depth of his own nature.

Henry David Thoreau

The personality of a river is not to be found
in its water, nor its shape. The life of a river,
like that of a human being, consists in
the union of soul and body, the water
and the banks.

Henry Van Dyke

I marvel how the fishes live in the sea.
William Shakespeare

The seas are the heart's blood of the earth.
Henry Beston

I have been made to feel more at peace
about my hunting and fishing because of my
strict observance of conservation measures.
Jimmy Carter

The future lies in the strength with which
man can set his powers of creation against
his impulses for destruction. Perhaps this is
the unending frontier.
Marjory Stoneman Douglas

At the outset, the fact should be recognized
that the community of fishermen constitutes
a separate class or subrace among
the inhabitants of the earth.

Grover Cleveland

With appreciation of all the wonders
of nature to be seen, smelled, or heard on any
trip outdoors, the importance of the bag
grows less.

Ted Trueblood

The angling fever is a very real disease
and can only be cured by the application
of cold water and fresh, untainted air.

Theodore Gordon

The angler forgets most of the fish
he catches, but he does not forget the
streams and lakes in which they were caught.

Charles K. Fox

As the angler looks back, he thinks less
of individual captures and days than
of scenes in which he fished.

Lord Grey of Fallondon

Happiness is a blue sky, without clouds.

Alfred Hitchcock

One of the great qualities of fishing is
that it is non-competitive.

John Atherton

To compete against another angler
is to do so once removed and always
on an unequal basis.

Russell Chatham

Fishing is a constant
reminder of the democracy
of life, of humility, and of
human frailty. The forces
of nature discriminate
for no man.

Herbert Hoover

If you instill in your child a love
of the outdoors and an appreciation of nature,
you will have given him a treasure
no one can take away.

Ted Trueblood

Let children walk with Nature.

John Muir

Many of the most highly publicized events
of my presidency are not nearly as
memorable or significant in my life
as fishing with my daddy.

Jimmy Carter

Nature never did betray
The heart that loved her.

William Wordsworth

Every country boy
is entitled to a creek.

Havilah Babcock

There is certainly something in angling
that tends to produce a gentleness of spirit
and a pure serenity of mind.

Washington Irving

Fishing is much more than fish.
Fishing is the great occasion when we may
return to the fine simplicity of our forefathers.

Herbert Hoover

It is difficult to talk to
people who are not
particularly interested
in the value of a river.

Zane Grey

My advice is go often and visit
many localities. Kill no more fish than you
require for your own eating, and do that
in the most scientific manner.

Charles Bradford

Throw the little ones back.

Fisherman's Saying

Catch no more fish than you can salt.

Fisherman's Saying

A good game fish is too valuable to be caught only once.

Lee Wulff

The fish is not so much
your quarry
as your partner.

Arnold Gingrich

LESSON 6: SILENCE
Quiet Waters Are Wise Counsel

The angler, whether he admits it or not, seeks something more important than his daily limit. He seeks a sense of calm that is as much a part of fishing as hooks and bait. In 1653, Izaak Walton wrote, "God never did make a more calm, quiet, innocent recreation than angling." Even in the relative calm of the 1600s, the joy of fishing stemmed, in part, from man's natural attraction to silence. At its best, angling is a contemplative sport, providing the fisherman with ample opportunity to sort through the fleeting problems of the day.

The most successful fishing trips are not judged by the size of the catch. The lucky angler captures more than fish; he also recaptures a sense of perspective born from the wise counsel of quiet waters.

We need the tonic of wilderness.

Henry David Thoreau

There is certainly
something in fishing
that tends to produce
a gentleness of spirit and
a pure sincerity of mind.

Washington Irving

The music of angling is more compelling
to me than anything contrived
in the greatest symphony hall.

A. J. McClane

Nature is a gentle guide.

Montaigne

Never does nature say one thing
and wisdom another.

Juvenal

In its deepest self, fishing is the most solitary
sport, for at its best it is all between you
and the fish.

Arnold Gingrich

Next to prayer, fishing is the most personal relationship of man.

Herbert Hoover

As civilization, cement pavements,
office buildings and radio have overwhelmed
us, the need for regeneration has increased.
Fishing is a sound, valid reason to go away
from here to somewhere else.

Herbert Hoover

Fishing is more than a sport.
It is a way of thinking and doing, a way of
reviving the mind and body.

Roderick Haig-Brown

Fishing is not so much getting fish as it is
a state of mind, a lure for the human soul
into refreshment.

Herbert Hoover

By common consent, fishing is the most
peaceful of all forms of sport.

H. T. Sheringham

Take rest.
A field that has rested
gives a beautiful crop.

Ovid

The fisherman loves to row out
in the stillness of the mists of the morning
when the lake is like polished black glass.

Ernest Lyons

The banks of a river are frequented by
a strange company and are full of mysterious
sounds — the cluck and laughter of water,
the piping of birds, the hum of insects and
the whispering of wind in the willows.

Roland Pertwee

We all sprang from common ancestors who
lived their lives in silence that was broken
only by the sounds of nature. Every human
being has an atavistic need for silence.

Ted Trueblood

Surely one of the richest bounties of angling
is to grow deeply intimate with the inner life
of the world of nature, and in so doing,
to come closer to your deepest self.

Nick Lyons

Silence is the element in which great things
fashion themselves together.

Maurice Maeterlinck

What is empathic in angling is made so by
the long silences — the unproductive periods.

Thomas McGuane

As line spins off the reel of life, the years
weave a crazy quilt pattern. And it is strange
how the seemingly great things become small
and the small things become great.

Ralph Bandini

A fisherman must be of contemplative
   mind, for it is a long time between bites.

Herbert Hoover

Fishing makes you think.

Fisherman's Saying

Many men go fishing all of their lives
   without knowing that it is not fish
      they are after.

Henry David Thoreau

I never found a companion that was
so companionable as solitude.
Henry David Thoreau

Speech is of time, silence is of eternity.
Thomas Carlyle

Discover creative solitude.
Carl Sandburg

Fishing at its most rudimentary level
is essentially solitary.
Russell Chatham

God is the friend of silence.
Mother Teresa

Then come, my friend, forget your foes,
    and leave your fears behind,
    And wander forth to try your luck
    with a cheerful, quiet mind.

                              Henry Van Dyke

Quiet places should be enjoyed.
    Save the quiet places first.

                              Ernest Lyons

It is neither wealth nor splendor,
    but tranquility and occupation
    which give happiness.

                            Thomas Jefferson

Never give up listening
to the sounds of birds.

John James Audubon

Fishing: The solitary and friendly sport.

R. Palmer Baker, Jr.

I have often regretted my speech,
　　　　never my silence.

Publilius Syrus

Silence is a friend who will never betray.

Confucius

Silence is full of potential wisdom.

Aldous Huxley

Don't talk unless you can improve
　　　　the silence.

New England Saying

A fish wouldn't get caught if it kept its mouth shut.

Fisherman's Saying

Someone just back of you
while you are fishing is as
bad as someone looking
over your shoulder
while you write
a letter to your girl.

Ernest Hemingway

LESSON 7: HUMILITY

You Can't Hook 'Em All

Benjamin Disraeli correctly observed, "There is no education like adversity." Had he been a fisherman, he might have added, "There is no education like an empty catch-net."

Fishing is a humbling sport. Even the most seasoned angler must, from time to time, relearn the lessons that only failure can teach.

Inevitably, we learn more about ourselves in times of trouble than we do in times of plenty. And so it is with fishing. On the following pages, we consider the wisdom of humility as seen through the eyes of the fisherman.

Fisherman's luck means that the time,
the place, the fish and you are all together.
It does not happen very often.

Zane Grey

He who has never failed somewhere,
that man cannot be great.

Herman Melville

Humility neither falls far, nor heavily.

Publilius Syrus

Wisdom is often times nearer when we stoop
than when we soar.

William Wordsworth

The skillful angler
must be full of
humble thoughts.

Gervase Markham

No matter how good
a man gets at fishing,
he'll never land every
fish he hooks.

A. J. McClane

There was never an
angler who lived but that
there was a fish capable
of taking the conceit
out of him.

Zane Grey

Nothing sets a person so far out
of the devil's reach as humility.

Jonathan Edwards

Be completely humble and gentle;
be patient, bearing with one another in love.

Ephesians 4:2

God resists the proud, and gives grace
to the humble.

I Peter 5:5

Pride is surely the most unbecoming
of all vices in a fisherman.

Henry Van Dyke

It is not a fish until it is on the bank.

Irish Proverb

Bragging may not bring happiness,
    but no man having caught a large fish,
      goes home through the alley.

Anonymous

Into each life some rain must fall,
    some days must be dark and dreary.
Henry Wadsworth Longfellow

Before honor is humility.
Proverbs 15:33

Older anglers know that misfortune is but
a proper contrast to the good days astream.
A. J. McClane

A fish on the hook is better
than ten in the brook.

Fisherman's Saying

It took me five seasons at Catalina
to catch a big tuna.

Zane Grey

He who is content to not-catch fish
will have his time and attention free for the
accumulation of a thousand experiences.

Sparse Grey Hackle

I can't believe one would enjoy one's kills very much without a nice percentage of misses.

T. H. White

Nothing grows faster than a fish from the time he bites until the time he gets away.

Fisherman's Saying

True humility is contentment.

Henri Frédéric Amiel

Lesson 8: Optimism

Cast Hope upon the Waters

Henry Ford once observed, "Whether you think you can or think you can't, you're right." This warning applies to all, but anglers are advised to pay special attention.

Fishing is a sport built upon hope. Each cast is made into uncertain waters, and the final outcome remains in doubt until the quarry is safely in the boat. Some days the fish aren't biting, and no angler on earth can make them rise to the bait. During such times, an optimistic spirit is more valuable than a box full of high-priced tackle.

The pessimist, focusing on his adversity and failures, soon loses hope and retires to the shore. He curses his bad luck, packs up his tackle box, and returns home empty-handed. But the optimistic angler, believing in the inevitability of his success, keeps casting. Eventually the tides turn, and the fish begin to bite.

In fishing, as in life, the size of the catch depends upon the size of one's hopes. On ponds, streams, rivers, lakes and oceans, the self-fulfilling prophesy is alive and well. And so are the fish.

The good angler must bring a large measure of hope and patience.

Izaak Walton

I know of no optimism so great
as that which perennially blooms in the heart
of a fisherman.

Burton L. Spiller

The happiness of your life depends
upon the quality of your thoughts;
therefore guard accordingly.

Marcus Aurelius

The charm of fishing is that it is
the pursuit of what is elusive but attainable,
a perpetual series of occasions for hope.

John Buchan

Hope deferred maketh the heart sick.

Proverbs 13:12

Great hopes make great men.

Thomas Fuller

Some fishermen see no fish and foolishly
believe that the river is empty.

Henry Van Dyke

I am an optimist. It does not seem too much
use being anything else.

Winston Churchill

Optimism is the faith that leads
to achievement. Nothing can be done
without hope and confidence.

Helen Keller

There are always greater fish than you
have caught, always the lure of greater task
and achievement, always the inspiration
to seek, to endure, to find.

Zane Grey

Fishermen are an optimistic class or they would not be fishermen.

Herbert Hoover

Fishing greats, whether they realize it or not,
practice PFA: Positive Fishing Approach.

Jim Chapralis

The biggest mistake most fishermen make
is that they give up too quickly. Some days
I fish four or five hours without finding
how to catch the fish, then catch the limit
in the next hour.

Ed Todtenbier

How keenly the love of angling is developed
in the bosoms of many men; how patient and
long suffering fishermen are, and how content
with the hope even of small mercies.

J. P. Wheeldon

All human wisdom is summed up in these
three words: wait and hope.

Alexandre Dumas

All things come to those who bait.

Fisherman's Saying

Experience usually is what you get
    when you don't get what you want, but if
there were no such thing as optimism, there
    wouldn't be any such thing as fishing.

Michael McIntosh

The pessimist sees the difficulty
    in every opportunity; the optimist sees
        the opportunity in every difficulty.

Lawrence Pearsall Jacks

You won't catch every fish you try for,
    but don't let that discourage you, because
        the best fishermen who ever lived
            can't do it either.

H. G. Tapply

Some anglers catch their best fish
            by the tale.

Fisherman's Saying

They are able who think they are able.

Virgil

I have never yet caught a fish on the first cast, nor have I ever made a first cast without thinking I would catch a fish.

Ellington White

So many fish. So little time.

Fisherman's Saying

He fishes on who catches one.

French Proverb

A fisherman is always hopeful — nearly always more hopeful than he has any right to be.

Roderick Haig-Brown

Every moment of life,
I suppose, is more or less
of a turning point.
Opportunities are
swarming around us
all the time thicker
than gnats at sundown.

Henry Van Dyke

The clearest sign of wisdom
is continued cheerfulness.

Montaigne

Happiness and misery depend as much
on temperament as on fortune.

La Rochefoucauld

Nothing is good or bad but thinking
makes it so.

William Shakespeare

Sadness is almost never anything
but a form of fatigue.

André Gide

Act as if it were impossible to fail.

Dorthea Brande

Bait the hook well; this fish will bite.

William Shakespeare

The pessimist complains about the wind;
the optimist expects it to change;
the realist adjusts the sails.

William Arthur Ward

Our life is what our thoughts make it.

Marcus Aurelius

The preposterous luck of a beginner
is well known to all fisherman.
It is an inexplicable thing.

Zane Grey

They can because they think they can.

Virgil

Lord, suffer me to catch
a fish so large that even I
in talking of it afterward
shall have no need to lie.

Suggested Motto:
Herbert Hoover's Fishing Lodge

Fishing is the eternal
Fountain of Youth.

Herbert Hoover

LESSON 9: GRATITUDE

Every Day Spent Fishing Is a Day To Give Thanks

Every day spent fishing should be a day of thanksgiving. Fishermen are surrounded by the beauty of nature, they experience the thrill of the catch, and they enjoy the companionship of fellow anglers. Even when the catch-net is empty, fishing is its own reward.

The following quotations celebrate the joy of angling. These words of wisdom prove once and for all that, in the world of fishing, there are no bad days.

There is always something wonderful about a new fishing adventure trip. Fishing is like Jason's quest for the Golden Fleece.

Zane Grey

When I first open my eyes upon
the morning meadows and look out upon
the beautiful world, I thank God I'm alive.

Ralph Waldo Emerson

The longer I live, the more beautiful
life becomes.

Frank Lloyd Wright

A thankful heart is not only the greatest
virtue, but the purest of all other virtues.

Cicero

Thanksgiving invites God to bestow
a second benefit.

Robert Herrick

To paraphrase a deceased patriot,
I regret that I have only one life to give
to my fly-fishing.

Robert Traver

Time is probably more generous
to the angler than to any other individual.
The wind, the sun, the open air, the colors
and smell, the loneliness of the sea or
the solitude of the stream,
work for some kind of magic.

Zane Grey

This time, like all times, is a very good one,
if we only know what to do with it.

Ralph Waldo Emerson

Fishing keeps us — part of us anyway —
boys forever.

Geoffrey Norman

As trauma and change rock your soul,
as you struggle to get that job or get through
college, no matter where you are, you can
always go fishing for something.

Mark Strand

I have laid aside business and gone a-fishing.

Izaak Walton

I don't want to sit at the head table anymore.
I want to go fishing.

George Bush

We fishermen dream far more often
of our favorite sport than other men dream
of theirs.

Will H. Dilg

Even the thousandth trip to the same old
familiar fished-out stream begins with
renewed hope, with unfailing faith.

Zane Grey

And this is no small thing, for in all its
history, angling has brought delight
to many and harm to no one.

Roderick Haig-Brown

The contentment which fills the mind
of the angler at the close of a day's sport is
one of the chiefest charms in his life.

Rev. William Cowper Prime

In our family, there was
no clear line between
religion and fly-fishing.

Norman Maclean

Why do I fish? The easiest answer is:
My father and all my ancestors
did it before me.

Jimmy Carter

The world of angling is richly diverse.
Carp fishing with dough balls in the Charles
River is no less within its realm than the
pursuit of giant marlin off the Morro.

Nick Lyons

Angling has this distinction of its own:
The very poorest man can, if he so chooses,
become a fisherman.

J. P. Wheeldon

Your headiest success as an angler
begins when you start caring more
about fishing than the fish.

Arnold Gingrich

Find the journey's end in every step.

Ralph Waldo Emerson

Begin at once to live and count each day
as a separate life.

Seneca

Old fishermen never die.
They just smell that way.

Fisherman's Saying

Anglers have a way of romanticizing their battles with fish.

Ernest Hemingway

The quicker a freshwater fish is on the fire
after he is caught, the better he is.

Mark Twain

I know of no fish that is improved by aging.
You can't cook a fish too soon.

Ted Trueblood

Oh, the brave Fisher's life.
It is the best of any,
'Tis full of pleasure, void of strife,
And 'tis belov'd of many.

Izaak Walton

It is not the fish we catch that counts,
  for they can be had for mere silver. It is
  the break of the waves, the joyous rush
  of the brook, and the contemplation
  of the eternal rush of the stream.

Herbert Hoover

The time must come to all of us,
  who live long, when memory is more than
  prospect. An angler who reaches this stage
  and reviews the pleasure of life will be
  grateful and glad he has been an angler.

Lord Grey of Fallondon

Sources

Anthony Acerrano 45
George Allen 79
Henri Frédéric Amiel 132
Donald Jack Anderson 64
Aristotle 38
John Ashley-Cooper 20
John Atherton 96
John James Audubon 117
St. Augustine 68
Havilah Babcock 99
R. Palmer Baker, Jr. 117
Honoré De Balzac 66
Ralph Bandini 113
Thomas Barker 39
Oa Battista 37
Tiny Bennett 38
Henry Beston 93
Roy Blount, Jr. 27
Charles Bradford 18, 102
Dorthea Brande 144
Jacob Bronowski 87
John Buchan 135
George Bush 153
Albert Camus 15
Thomas Carlyle 53, 115
Jimmy Carter 16, 59, 82, 86, 93, 98, 156
George Washington Carver 90
Cervantes 79
Jim Chapralis 49, 54, 138
Russell Chatham 96, 115
Winston Churchill 136
Cicero 151
Grover Cleveland 94
Confucius 54, 68, 118
Dante 83
Will H. Dilg 154
Benjamin Disraeli 54, 121

Marjory Stoneman Douglas 93
Alexandre Dumas 138
Thomas D'Urfey 26
Jonathan Edwards 126
Ralph Waldo Emerson 23, 34, 69, 79, 85, 151, 152, 157
Epictetus 66
Henry Ford 34, 58, 133
Charles K. Fox 18, 24, 78, 95
St. Frances of Sales 74
Ben Franklin 60, 74
Robert Frost 33, 34
Thomas Fuller 60, 75, 78, 135
André Gide 27, 144
Arnold Gingrich 20, 48, 74, 104, 108, 157
Theodore Gordon 33, 50, 94
Lord Grey of Fallondon 95, 160
Zane Grey 49, 50, 77, 81, 101, 122, 125, 129, 136, 146, 150, 152, 154
Palmer Hackle Esq. 26
Sparse Grey Hackle 19, 28, 58, 67, 129
Roderick Haig-Brown 21, 33, 57, 89, 110, 142, 154
Ernest Hemingway 120, 158
Heraclitus 36
Robert Herrick 151
Hippocrates 76, 85
Alfred Hitchcock 95
William Hjortsberg 56
Oliver Wendell Holmes 60
Herbert Hoover 23, 54, 55, 65, 86, 97, 100, 109, 110, 114, 137, 148, 160
William J. Hjortsberg 62
Ed Howe 18
Dave Hughes 36, 46
Aldous Huxley 118
Washington Irving 100, 107
Lawrence Pearsall Jacks 140
Thomas Jefferson 116

Sources

Samuel Johnson 24, 87
Wheeler Johnson 31
Joseph Joubert 72
Juvenal 108
Helen Keller 136
John Alden Knight 40
La Rochefoucauld 144
William Robinson Leigh 90
Henry Wadsworth Longfellow 128
Ernest Lyons 112, 116
Nick Lyons 77, 113, 156
Norman Maclean 155
Maurice Maeterlinck 113
Maimonides 31
J. J. Manley 84
Marcus Aurelius 87, 135, 146
Gervase Markham 123
Thomas Masaryck 91
A. J. McClane 32, 40, 71, 77, 108, 124, 128
Thomas McGuane 113
Michael McIntosh 140
Herman Melville 34, 122
Michelangelo 32
Montaigne 108, 144
John Trotwood Moore 78
John Muir 82, 98
Reinhold Niebuhr 76
Nietzsche 30
Geoffrey Norman 26, 32, 44, 48, 152
Thaddeus Norris 16
Ovid 42, 80, 111
Roland Pertwee 112
Rev. William Cowper Prime 154
Publilius Syrus 118, 122
Jack Randolph 58
John W. Randolph 20, 32, 62
Marjorie Kinnan Rawlings 86

George Reiger 38
Jean Jacques Rousseau 74
Archibald Rutledge 78
Carl Sandburg 77, 115
Seneca 30, 50, 85, 157
William Shakespeare 93, 144, 145
Herb Shriver 70
Solon 33
Sophocles 27, 31, 33
Burton L. Spiller 135
John Steinbeck 52
Dick Sternberg 36
Mark Strand 153
H. T. Sheringham 110
H. G. Tapply 140
Alfred Lord Tennyson 38
Mother Teresa 115
E. Donnall Thomas 25
Henry David Thoreau 23, 82, 85, 88, 90, 92, 106, 114, 115
Ed Todtenbier 138
Robert Traver 151
Ted Trueblood 21, 38, 41, 44, 87, 94, 98, 112, 159
Harry Truman 31
Mark Twain 159
Henry Van Dyke 61, 89, 92, 116, 126, 136, 143
Virgil 141, 146
Izaak Walton 17, 21, 23, 30, 34, 35, 68, 105, 134, 153, 159
William Arthur Ward 146
Charles F. Waterman 44, 48, 49
J. P. Wheeldon 138, 156
Ellington White 141
T. H. White 130
William Wordsworth 98, 122
Frank Lloyd Wright 151
Lee Wulff 103

About the Author

Criswell Freeman is a Doctor of Clinical Psychology living in Nashville, Tennessee. He is the author of *When Life Throws You a Curveball, Hit It* and *The Wisdom Series* from WALNUT GROVE PRESS. He is also a published country music songwriter.

About Wisdom Books

Wisdom Books chronicle memorable quotations in an easy-to-read style. Written by Criswell Freeman, this series provides inspiring, thoughtful and humorous messages from entertainers, athletes, scientists, politicians, clerics, writers and renegades. Each title focuses on a particular region or special interest.

Combining his passion for quotations with extensive training in psychology, Dr. Freeman revisits timeless themes such as perseverance, courage, love, forgiveness and faith.

"Quotations help us remember the simple yet profound truths that give life perspective and meaning," notes Freeman. "When it comes to life's most important lessons, we can all use gentle reminders."

The Wisdom Series
by Dr. Criswell Freeman

Wisdom Made In America
ISBN 1-887655-07-7

The Book of Southern Wisdom
ISBN 0-9640955-3-X

The Wisdom of the Midwest
ISBN 1-887655-17-4

The Book of Texas Wisdom
ISBN 0-9640955-8-0

The Book of Florida Wisdom
ISBN 0-9640955-9-9

The Book of California Wisdom
ISBN 1-887655-14-X

The Book of New England Wisdom
ISBN 1-887655-15-8

The Book of New York Wisdom
ISBN 1-887655-16-6

The Book of Country Music Wisdom
ISBN 0-9640955-1-3

The Wisdom of Old-Time Television
ISBN 1-887655-64-6

The Golfer's Book of Wisdom
ISBN 0-9640955-6-4

The Wisdom of Southern Football
ISBN 0-9640955-7-2

The Book of Stock Car Wisdom
ISBN 1-887655-12-3

The Wisdom of Old-Time Baseball
ISBN 1-887655-13-1

The Book of Football Wisdom
ISBN 1-887655-18-2

Wisdom Books are available through booksellers everywhere.
For information about a retailer near you, call 1-800-256-8584.